BRITAIN IN OLD PH

Blackheath

ANTHONY H. PAGE

With best wishes,
Anthony H Page

SUTTON PUBLISHING LIMITED

Sutton Publishing Limited
Phoenix Mill · Thrupp · Stroud
Gloucestershire · GL5 2BU

First published 2000

Title page photograph: The approach to Blackheath from Long Lane, *c.* 1910. On the left is the Ashley Hotel, with the spire of the Methodist church in the distance. (*Tony Taylor Collection*)

British Library Cataloguing in Publication Data
A catalogue record for this book is available from the British Library.

ISBN 0-7509-2562-0

Typeset in 10.5/13.5 Photina.
Typesetting and origination by
Sutton Publishing Limited.
Printed in Great Britain by
J.H. Haynes & Co. Ltd, Sparkford.

(*Tony Taylor collection*)

CONTENTS

	Introduction	5
1.	Scenes around Town	7
2.	Schools	31
3.	Shops & Pubs	37
4.	Churches & Chapels	55
5.	Work & Play	81
6.	People & Events	103
	Acknowledgements	127

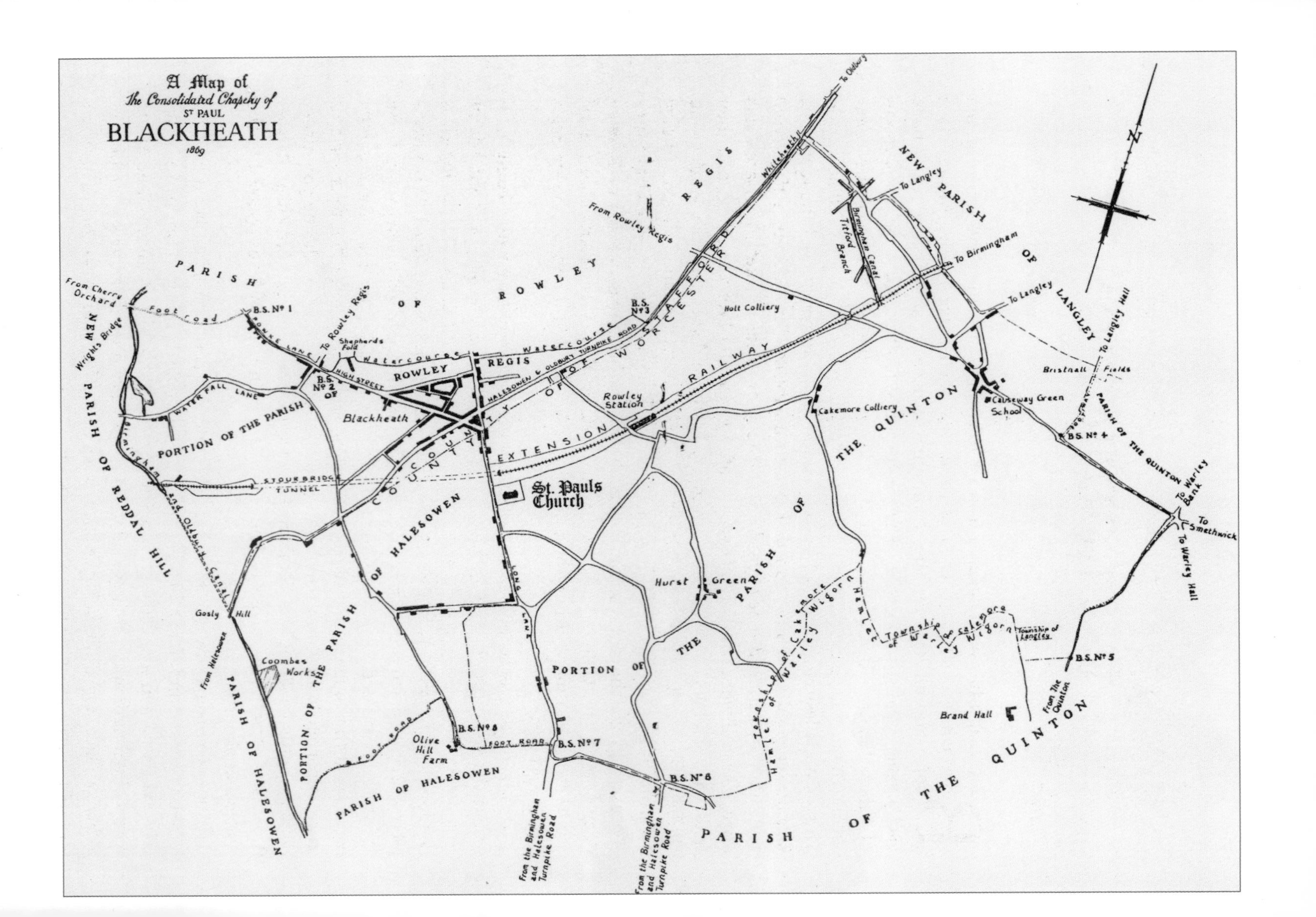
A Map of
The Consolidated Chapelry of
St PAUL
BLACKHEATH
1869
N
PARISH OF ROWLEY REGIS
NEW PARISH OF LANGLEY
PARISH OF THE QUINTON
PARISH OF THE QUINTON
PORTION OF THE PARISH OF THE QUINTON
PORTION OF THE PARISH OF HALESOWEN
PORTION OF THE PARISH OF HALESOWEN
PARISH OF HALESOWEN
PARISH OF HALESOWEN
NEW PARISH OF REDDAL HILL
PORTION OF THE PARISH OF ROWLEY REGIS
COUNTY OF WORCESTER
RAILWAY EXTENSION
St. Pauls Church
Blackheath
ROWLEY REGIS
High Street
Watercourse
Halesowen & Oldbury Turnpike Road
Waterfall Lane
Powke Lane
Long Lane
Foot road
Stourbridge Tunnel
Birmingham and Oldbury Canal
Birmingham Canal
Titford Branch
Whiteheath
To Oldbury
To Langley
To Birmingham
To Langley Hall
To Warley Bank
To Smethwick
To Warley Hall
To Rowley Regis
From Rowley Regis
From Cherry Orchard
Wrights Bridge
From Halesowen
From the Birmingham and Halesowen Turnpike Road
From the Birmingham and Halesowen Turnpike Road
From The Quinton
Shephards Fold
Holt Colliery
Cakemore Colliery
Rowley Station
Causeway Green School
Bristnall Fields
Hurst Green
Gosly Hill
Coombes Works
Olive Hill Farm
Brand Hall
Hamlet of Cakemore
Township of Warley Wigorn
Hamlet of Cakemore
Township of Warley Wigorn
Township of Langley
B.S. No 1
B.S. No 2
B.S. No 3
B.S. No 4
B.S. No 5
B.S. No 6
B.S. No 7
B.S. No 8

INTRODUCTION

Blackheath has been called a frontier town, and in many ways this is an apt description, situated as it is (and has been since its beginnings as a separate entity) at the boundary between administrations, both ecclesiastical and governmental. The geographical limits adopted for the purposes of this collection include most of the old postal district of Blackheath, near Birmingham, which approximates to the Anglican parish of St Paul's, Blackheath. This more or less conforms to local recognition of what constituted the township, despite repeated reorganisation of local authority control. Although the actual boundary has moved a few yards over the years, the Market Place area has always been divided, initially between Staffordshire and Worcestershire, and then with successive local government changes, firstly in 1966, between Warley and Dudley County Boroughs, and later, in 1974, between Sandwell and Dudley Metropolitan Boroughs. A similar demarcation existed in parliamentary representation, the area being shared between the constituencies of Rowley Regis/Tipton and Oldbury/Halesowen, followed by Warley West and Halesowen/Stourbridge, and more latterly by being linked for the first time into Rowley Regis and Halesowen.

It is generally acknowledged that Blackheath did not come into being as a residential area until the 1830s, and only developed its own identity with the advent of industry and commerce. It was, and to a large extent still is, a working-class community, and an examination of the Trade Directories of the mid-1800s reveals plenty of quarrymen and miners; together with the home-based nailing trade, these industries accounted for most of the work opportunities in the area. There is little evidence at this time of the professional classes, and it is assumed that their services were imported from Rowley or Halesowen. A similar trawl of the neighbouring parish records confirms this demographic picture; the registers of St Giles, Rowley Regis, start mentioning baptisms and marriages from the 'Town' as opposed to the 'Village' at about the same time.

It has been suggested that Blackheath's name was derived from earlier references to 'Bleak Heath' and 'Blake Heath', and on early maps it is shown on the toll road between Halesowen and Oldbury; apart from the odd hostelry there was little in the way of dwelling-houses or shops. As the name implies, the district was something of a dreary place, especially in the winter or following bouts of prolonged rain, when most of the area was little more than a swamp.

The parish of St Paul was formed in 1865. By this time Blackheath's population had grown to some 5,400, and it was felt that it needed its own parish church, so that people no longer had to travel to Rowley, Quinton, Halesowen or Oldbury. (The parish boundaries are shown on the map on page 4.) The new church was consecrated in 1869. Several nonconformist chapels also sprang up, and by the early decades of the twentieth century two Methodist Circuits, the Baptists, the Congregationalists and the Salvation Army were all well established. Evidence of their activities is contained within these pages.

Blackheath soon became a 'boom town', and, with an eye for good business – one of the characteristics of Black Country folk – many people eagerly took advantage of the opportunities presented firstly by the abundance of natural resources in the quarries and mines, and later, after the coming of the railway in 1867, by the rapidly expanding industrial developments. The largest factory to make its mark was the Excelsior Works of T.W. Lench, followed by British Thompson Houston. As industry thrived, so the mines declined, and the last working pit closed down in 1919.

Many pictures in this book are taken from family albums, because there are few official pictorial records. Perhaps this reflects the nature of the population, for whom cameras would have been a rare luxury. Most of the population still lived in overcrowded conditions, cramped terraced houses or small cottages, but many homes were converted into public houses or shops, and the well-stocked shops gave the impression of prosperity.

But the Blackheath folk of yesteryear were characterised by all the desirable traits of good Black Country stock: they were hard-working, honest, dependable, never too busy to lend a hand, and always ready to help those in need. But their lives were not glamorous; many of them endured abject poverty and coped with hardships unknown in today's Britain. Nevertheless there are people in Blackheath today in their eighties and nineties who still live in the same house in which they, and perhaps their parents and even grandparents, were born and lived before them. Many of the family businesses still exist and are run by direct descendants of their founders.

Without these folk, this book could not have come into being, and it is hoped that the pictures contained herein reflect all the various aspects of the history of our town. If anyone reading this book has any old photographs or other memorabilia that they are willing to loan for use in future publications, please contact the author via the publishers.

1

Scenes around Town

The Market Place in the mid-1960s, looking towards High Street from the county boundary between Rowley Regis (Staffordshire) and Halesowen (Worcestershire). The controversial subway, originally a deep air raid shelter, with the public conveniences can be clearly seen, while two-way traffic continues to use High Street, causing the endless bottle-necks which led to the construction of the first phase of the ring road development. (*Author*)

This 1904 view from Long Lane towards Birmingham Road shows the old cottages and shops situated behind the Royal Oak public house, including the dwelling of Mrs Southall, and the fish and chip shop owned by Mr Gerry Westwood. Children are happily playing in the middle of the road and the shop owner is resting on the front steps as she awaits customers. The squat tower of St Giles's parish church can be seen in the distance. (*Ken Rock Collection*)

Long Lane, July 1961. Behind the trees in the centre of the picture stands the large house that was formerly the home of the Pittaway family, and later became Lingard's, a clothing manufacturer, employing many women as seamstresses. The Travellers Rest public house and the Ashley Hotel are on the left, while on the extreme right the awning of the Kings Cinema is just visible. Note the sign pointing down Avenue Road to the station. (*Derek Crump*)

The King's Cinema, Long Lane, 1932. Owned and operated by Mr T. Cooper, this was the favourite location of many courting couples, but care had to be taken because the management would stand no nonsense. Any untoward behaviour or excessive noise would result in (at the least) a gentle prod from the stick kept for the purpose by Mr Cooper himself. Saturday morning matinees were the staple diet for Blackheath youngsters, and taught them a great deal about the wider world. (*Harry Brettle*)

The Market Place, *c.* 1950. This traction engine, one of the last to be seen in town, is making its slow way around the traffic island. (*Tony Taylor Collection*)

The Market Place, looking from Halesowen Street towards Oldbury Road, in the early 1920s. The Royal Oak public house is on the right. On the left are The Shambles, Mr E. Alsopp's shoe shop and Mr W. Parkes's hardware shop. The Shoulder of Mutton public house and the Handel Hotel stand on either side of the entrance to Birmingham Road. (*Fred Darby*)

Long Lane, looking towards Malt Mill Lane, 1917. The junctions with Church Street and Green Lane are both visible in this postcard view. A photographer was obviously an unusual sight to judge by the expressions of these children; even the local policeman taking up his station at the bottom of Vicarage Road looks interested. The entrance gates to St Paul's Church are on the left, with the vicarage garden on the right. (*Ken Rock Collection*)

Birmingham Road, looking towards Rowley village, *c.* 1912. The large house just beyond the church was removed to make way for a garage, while the larger housing in the middle distance gave way to the new council estate. The two carts making their way up Rowley Hill are just passing the Sir Robert Peel public house. (*Ken Rock Collection*)

This cottage in Oldbury Road is one of the oldest remaining houses still occupied in Blackheath. The deeds show that it was built in the late eighteenth century, and had 26 acres of ground. Mr E.H. Careless lived here from about 1920 and together with his two sons looked after the gardens, from which they ran a garden centre and nursery. (*Dennis Careless*)

Birmingham Road, looking towards Market Place from Regis Road, 1950s. The South Staffs Garage (originally Harper's) on the corner of Causeway is seen receiving a delivery of petrol. Behind the trees and fence on the extreme right was the British Restaurant, built following the Second World War to provide nourishing food at reasonable prices. It only lasted a few years, however, and the building was taken over by Pye Telecommunications. (*Christopher Willetts*)

Mincing Lane in the 1920s, when it still retained a rural atmosphere. Looking down from Bell End towards Oldbury Road the only development to the left appears to be a farmhouse, with a solitary house on the corner of Pencricket Lane on the bottom right. (*Christopher Willetts*)

The High Street, *c.* 1912. This view is from the junction with Ross, looking towards the town centre. The passing point for the trams can be seen outside the Royal Exchange public house, with the tower of High Street Methodist church in the middle distance. Mrs Agnes Nock was the proprietor of the sweet shop on the corner, and her daughter recalls that they had to stay open each evening until the last tram had passed, as the driver always called in for a packet of twist. (*M. Parkes*)

Further down High Street, looking down towards the Market Place, mid-1930s. The horse-drawn cart is waiting outside what was to become F.W. Woolworth's, opposite a shop (Parkes Bros?) advertising tennis rackets and balls. F.W. Boswell's boots and shoes store occupies the premises on the left. (*Ken Rock Collection*)

The High Street, mid-1950s. This picture was taken outside T.P. Moyle's shop, with the Belisha beacon prominent. Woolworth's has now arrived, and the covered market hall is very much the same as it is today. The one-way system is not yet in operation, as can be seen from the Standard Vanguard making its way up the road. (*Ann Harris*)

The High Street, pictured from the George and Dragon public house, *c.* 1950. The shops are (from left to right) a fish and chip shop, Westwood's newsagents, Gaunt's funeral parlour and Hobbs's builders merchants, whose premises were on the corner of Causeway, then accessible to through traffic. On the right-hand side, on the corner of Darby Street, is George Cooke's corn and seed merchants, next to High Street Methodist Church, with its war memorial. (*C.H.A.S.*)

The name betraying its pastoral origins, this is Shepherd's Fold being demolished in the late 1950s to make way for more modern housing. This photograph was taken from opposite the George and Dragon public house. The building on the right was the public convenience. (*Derek Crump*)

These fine parlour-type houses in Station Road, pictured here in 1912, were considered to be among the more desirable houses in the town in the early part of the twentieth century. The road runs between Long Lane and the station, parallel to the railway line, and it was later renamed Avenue Road. (*Kath Mole*)

Rowley Regis and Blackheath station, 1918. It was evidently a busy time, as crowds are gathered on both platforms, awaiting the departure of the train. The coal yard and goods marshalling area are on the left. (*Barbara Holmes*)

Some of the last terraced houses to be redeveloped were these in Darby Street, which had stood for almost a century. This view was taken in 1985 from the Beeches Road end, looking towards High Street, with the premises of B. Hobbs visible at the end. (*Roy Horton*)

The junction in Long Lane, which became known as Shell Corner (the shell which gave rise to the name being clearly visible on the traffic island), pictured *c.* 1930. Long Lane continues on the left, with Nimmings Road branching off to the right. The properties were built on part of 'Bowlers Meadow'; on a plan dated 13 February 1903 the owner of the meadow was given as Jos. Parkes, Esq. (*Valerie Lloyd*)

This postcard, captioned 'The Nimmings', gives another view of the junction, looking up Long Lane from Blackheath town centre, again *c.* 1930. On the left John Townsend is attending to his shop window, while F. Honeysett & Son's bakery stands beyond the junction. (*Valerie Lloyd*)

Before the laying of a new sewer and drainage system, Shell Corner was frequently troubled by floods during periods of rainfall, and here we see an intrepid motorist negotiating the island on 14 June 1931, watched by members of the Honeysett family. Their confectionery was renowned throughout the area for its quality, but Ernest recalls that the cellar and storage areas were often under water, no doubt adding to the flavour! (*Ernest Honeysett*)

Oldbury Road, looking towards the town centre, late 1970s. From right to left the buildings are the Railway Inn, Horace Perks, barber, with his distinctive red and white rotating pole, Patrick's ladies' wear, Smith & Hiscock's decorating supplies and L.E. Payne's gentlemen's outfitters. These shops were all demolished not long after this photograph was taken to make way for the ring road. (*Ron Wood*)

A report in the *County Express*, dated 1841, stated that Blackheath had become a 'Boom Coal Mining Town', with pits springing up around the area, welcoming miners from many parts of the country. Named because of its proximity to the railway, the Station Colliery was one of many which provided work for the incoming miners. The chimney-stack was visible for miles, as was the pit bank, and transportation of the mined coal was simply undertaken via the goods depot at Blackheath station. (*Tony Taylor Collection*)

With the opening of the Stourbridge Extension Railway in 1867, a new portion of track from Old Hill to Galton Junction in Smethwick made possible through journeys from Worcester to Birmingham, and thence by connection to all parts of the United Kingdom. The pit bank is just visible on the left in this postcard from the early 1930s. There are few passengers about but a fully laden goods train with full steam up is awaiting departure. (*Ken Rock Collection*)

By the 1970s there was no evidence left of the colliery and the site was taken over for a more up-to-date fuel, as Shell opened their petroleum distribution depot here. The huge tanks tower over the roof of the station. (*Ron Wood*)

Park Street, 1973. A.S. Price, wholesale chemist, occupies the building on the left, with the Salvation Army Citadel as its neighbour. At the top of the road on the left, where it meets Long Lane, is the King's Theatre building with John Sturman's corn mill on the right. (*C.H.A.S.*)

The yard and workshop of Dallows Monumental Ltd backed on to the railway embankment at the top of Avenue Road, at the junction with Long Lane. It is pictured here in 1973, just before closure. (*Ron Wood*)

Halesowen Street, with the Rex cinema on the right. Opened in 1938, the cinema was described as a non-combine, privately owned Super Cinema, able to offer patrons select programmes of their choice. Picture-goers waiting for the second house could pop across the road for refreshment at one of two public houses, the Beech Tree and the Vine. Waiting at the bus stop is the Midland Red service 217 from Oldbury to Halesowen. (*Harry Brettle*)

With the advent of television, the Rex soon lost out and ended its life as a popular bingo hall. The bus stop remains, as does the Beech Tree public house, but the cinema is about to be demolished to make way for the new Sainsbury's store. (*Christopher Willetts*)

Houses and shops in Birmingham Road, awaiting redevelopment in the 1970s. The Candy Spot has just closed, as has Cashmores, but W. Holmes (newsagent), F. Darby (grocer) and Mr Levett (butcher) are still trading. (*Ron Wood*)

Powke Lane and Netherton, photographed from Lench's Recreation Grounds in the mid-1920s. The gun was given to the town for services rendered by the people of Blackheath in the First World War. In the distance is the Rowley Regis gas works, surrounded by other industrial concerns. The war memorial, which then stood in isolation, is now incorporated into the cemetery on the same site. (*Ken Rock Collection*)

Powke Lane and the war memorial, before any residential building took place. The wall on the right remains, although the fencing has long since been replaced. (*Ken Rock Collection*)

Two views of Beeches Road in 1915, from the junction with Holly Road (above) and from John Street (below). Previously called Tump Road, it was described at the time as one of the leafiest residential areas of the town. The recently planted beech trees gave the street, and the public house at the junction with Halesowen Street, their names. (*Tony Taylor and Ken Rock Collections*)

The Blackheath branch library in Carnegie Road, pictured in 1969. It was opened on 16 February 1909. (*C.H.A.S.*)

As the population increased, so did the need for housing, and a large council development began in the mid-1920s, mostly on virgin soil on both sides of Birmingham Road towards Rowley Church. Typical of the estates was Regis Road, seen here from the junction with Birmingham Road, with Limes Avenue going off to the right, in about 1937. The houses offered tenants modern kitchens, inside toilets and bathrooms, and must have seemed luxurious compared with some of the properties from which they were rehoused. (*Fred Darby*)

Oldbury Road at Whiteheath, pictured in the mid-1950s before road widening, modernisation and the building of the Catholic church. Boys are playing on the water pipes which were waiting to be laid to carry the stream under the road; behind them is an open view back towards Rowley and 'the quack', playground for scores of youngsters over the years. The summit of Turner's Hill can be seen over the mounds of earth. The annual funfair was held here at the junction with Throne Road. (*Len Waters*)

Holly Road at the junction with Beeches Road, 1905. A tram glides past the onlookers on its way to Old Hill, via Perry Park Road (commonly known as The Tump). (*Tony Taylor Collection*)

Perry Park Road, viewed from the waste ground at Highfield Road looking towards Netherton, mid-1950s. The railway tunnel passes beneath these fields on its way from Old Hill to Blackheath. This was also the route followed by the tramway, because the bends in the road were easier than the much steeper slope of Waterfall Lane. (*Amy Bussey*)

This back-fold of a house in Heath Street is typical of much of the housing stock at the beginning of the twentieth century. Here were located the brewhouse, the privy and the washhouse, and in many cases a pig sty or chicken run. It would also contain a workshop in which the women of the house would engage in nailmaking or similar pursuits to enable a slightly higher standard of living. (*Ron Wood*)

Darby Street, pictured from the tower of High Street Methodist Church in June 1993, looking towards Beeches Road. The roof of the Cave Adullam Baptist Church is visible on the skyline (*Christopher Willetts*)

Part of Birmingham Road just before redevelopment in the mid-1970s. The large shop, already abandoned, on the corner of George Avenue was formerly the premises of Graham Bonner, who traded as a photographer (and eventually worked on the staff of the *County Express*). Mrs Doreen Bonner also sold baby goods including prams, and a good range of model-making equipment. Other shops shown here include Tuc-Tin (fancy goods) and Mary Woodall (ladies' hairdressing). (*Ron Wood*)

The High Street photographed from the junction with Halesowen Street in 1905. On the left is the premises of Hobbs & Son, general dealers. This described itself as the 'Original Cheap Shop', and sold many items from lamp oil to suitcases, usually displayed on the pavement. The original Moyle's grocer's shop is on the right. (*Ken Rock Collection*)

A general view of Britannia Park, *c.* 1935. The first Sons of Rest building and the bowling green are in the foreground. The houses in the distance are in Mackmillan Road, and the chimney of the brickworks is just visible beyond. (*Derek Crump*)

The corner shop and adjacent cottages at the junction of Holly Road and Powke Lane, awaiting demolition in 1969. (*C.H.A.S.*)

2

Schools

Mr J.L. Johnson, head teacher of Rowley Regis Boys' School. The school was based in Powke Lane from 1918 to 1932, when it moved to new premises in Britannia Road. Mr Johnson oversaw the move, but retired shortly afterwards. He was replaced by George Alfred Willetts, who remained as head for many years. (*Alan Atkinson*)

There have been school premises in Powke Lane for well over a century, with a variety of names, including the National School, County Infant and Primary, and Senior School, but many people still regard it as the 'Board School'. The school celebrated its centenary in 1987, when former pupils, teachers and parents held a festival week. (*Denise McDonald*)

Blackheath County Primary Junior Mixed School (Powke Lane) football team, 1949/50, winners of the 'T.B. Williams Cup'. Back row, left to right: Mr Beasley, Mr Richards, Mr Willetts. Middle row: J. Homer, C. Millinchip, C. Bagley, E. Baker, D. Westwood, J. Lenton. Front row: A. Green, A. Mitchell, W. Potter (captain), J. Blakeway, D. Hale. (*Denise McDonald*)

Pupils of Holt Road Junior School enjoying a trip to London in 1958. They had a guided tour of the Houses of Parliament, escorted by the Member of Parliament for Oldbury and Halesowen, Mr Arthur Moyle. Some of the teachers involved are Mr Brittain, Mr Portman, Mr Cox and Mrs Barnsley. (*Kath Mole*)

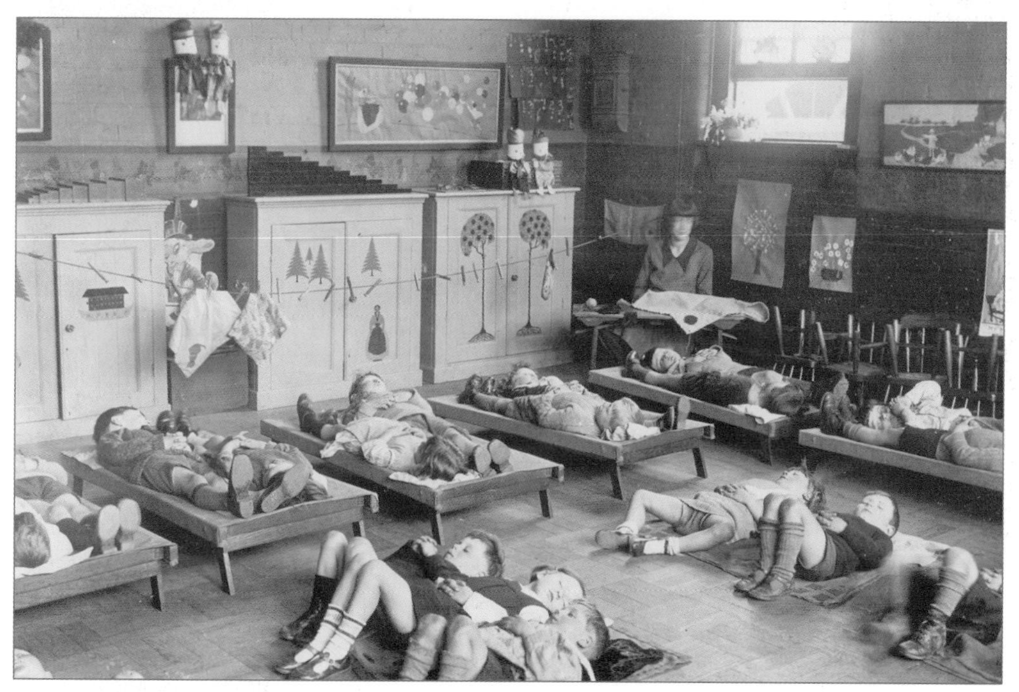

Peace descends on an afternoon class at Causeway Green Junior School in 1928, when the pupils have to take their compulsory sleeping period after lunch. (*Margaret Andersson*)

The class at the Church of England Infant School, 1929. (*Margaret Andersson*)

A patriotic gymnastic display on the sports field of Britannia Road Boys' School in the early 1950s. The houses in Habberley Road are beyond the playing field, with the distinctive chimney-stack of the Rowley Regis Brick Company in Oldbury Road just behind them. (*Alan Atkinson*)

Britannia Road Boys' School boxing team, 1954/5. The school had a very good record for sporting activities, particularly the boxing team, whose members competed against other schools in the area. Many of the team members went on to obtain honours in amateur boxing throughout the country. Back row, left to right: Mr Williams, ? Hughes, M. Newman, B. Harris, ? Capewell, N. Hill, -?-, ? Walters, Mr Walton. Front row: K. Locke, -?-, -?-, -?-, S. Hayes, Mr G.A. Willetts, -?-, -?-, -?-, E. Locke. (*Morris Newman*)

Alderman George Palmer JP, CC, Mayor of Rowley Regis, presenting books to the value of £3 to Terrance Grant, after he came second in a competition to design a poster for UNESCO. The competition was organised by Staffordshire Education Committee. The presentation took place at Rowley Regis County Secondary School on 3 November 1949. (*Alan Atkinson*)

Form 3B of Beeches Road School adopting a rather glum attitude for the cameraman for the annual school photograph in 1933. (*Frank Wyle*)

Members of Blackheath Junior School pictured in Britannia Park on Friday 20 July 1973, after making their contribution to the national 'Plant a Tree in '73' campaign. The newly constructed sports pavilion is the building is immediately behind them, with the new Sons of Rest headquarters at the rear behind the bowling green. (*County Express*)

3

Shops & Pubs

One of the oldest and most important public houses in the area was the Royal Oak, situated almost halfway between Oldbury and Halesowen on the toll road. It is not known when the first hostelry was built on this site, but certainly it has its history in the early part of the nineteenth century or before. It remained in the ownership of the Darby family for many years, and it is believed that this picture dates from the early 1900s. (*Fred Darby*)

Joseph (left) and Enoch Eley, posing in front of an impressive display of meat, 1910. Their shop, at the lower end of High Street, remains as a family business to the present day, but doubtless the European regulations would frown on such an unhygienic method of display. (*Philip Bannister*)

The Handel Hotel, at the corner of Birmingham Road and Oldbury Road, was the terminus for the trams, where the line comes to an abrupt end. These carters, posing for the photographer in about 1900, were probably council workers, the early equivalent of our refuse collectors. The building adjacent to the hotel in Oldbury Road was the Hippodrome, where many local entertainers performed for their peers. (*Edgar Smith*)

C.R. Hancox ran a popular wholesale tobacconist and sweet shop from these premises next to the King's Cinema in Long Lane. Pictured here in the mid-1930s, the firm's delivery van and extensive window display are evocative of the age. (*Author's Collection*)

Shops in Birmingham Road, early 1900s. These two shops stood a few doors away from the Shoulder of Mutton, and belonged at various times to the Rose and Adams families. Behind the shops, through the archway, was the original mill belonging to the Sturman family (part of which remains today as a food outlet, behind Barclays Bank). The goods on display in the window included fresh fruit and vegetables and home-made lemonade. (*David Taylor*)

A steam-driven lorry delivers supplies from the City Brewery, Lichfield, to the New Inn in Oldbury Road. Landlord William Bennion is shown with the delivery men, and the lady with the baby is his daughter Edna. These premises were demolished and a new pub built in the late 1920s. (*Colin Wood*)

The owner and staff of Blackheath post office, *c.* 1900. According to the contemporary Ordnance Survey map, it was situated a few doors lower down High Street than the present post office. Left to right: F. Sturman, J.P. Dallow (postmaster), Mrs Dallow, Mrs Nicklin, ? Smith, W. Smith, C. Tromans, G. Tromans. (*Frank Wyle*)

Walter F. Taylor was the proprietor of Gorsty Hill post office, and also ran a business as an electrical engineer. These premises, seen here in the late 1940s, have now been demolished, with the replacement post office being situated on the opposite side of the road. Note the old GR letter-box in the wall behind the firm's van. (*Iris Dickens*)

Priest's electrical shop has been a feature of the Market Place for over eighty years. Originally a single-fronted shop, it expanded into the former fish and chip shop next door to provide more spacious accommodation for the growing stock of consumer items. The shop front underwent a face-lift in the 1950s, and the latest washing machines, vacuum cleaners, televisions, radios and record players are clearly displayed. (*Bob Priest*)

An impression of how the town centre might have appeared in earlier days is given by this lovely watercolour painting of the Royal Oak public house. The artist's name is not known, but it was believed to have been painted in the late 1790s. Note the Georgian-style windows, and the absence of development to the left of the pub. (*Fred Darby*)

The Townsend family posing outside their shop on Shell Corner in 1913. Left to right: John Horace, Lydia Ann (née Judd), baby Frank and John. The plans for the shop were drawn up by William & Bloomer of Old Hill in October 1910 and the premises were built in 1911. The advertising poster in the left-hand window invites patrons to a twice-nightly contest between man and beast, featuring convict number 113, with admission prices ranging between 2*d* and 6*d*. (*Valerie Lloyd*)

A 1916 advertisement for the draper's shop of W. Darby (Connop), which was situated on the corner of Market Place and Halesowen Street, and described itself as 'the People's Choice'. (*Fred Darby*)

The Manchester House, 1937. This Mitchells & Butlers public house was situated on the corner of Heath Street and High Street. Shortly after this photograph was taken it was demolished to make way for the present building. (*C.H.A.S.*)

John Sturman came to Blackheath from Crick in Northamptonshire and first set up in business in Birmingham Road. As trade prospered the family built the Victoria Corn Mill in Park Street in 1900. They remained the main corn dealers in the area, and at the end of rationing following the Second World War they still had over five hundred working horses registered on their books. (*Peter Hancox*)

The Darby family have run grocery stores for many years, and here we see Edna Darby serving in the shop in Birmingham Road. The personal service, wide range of goods stocked and home delivery were vital to the shop's success. (*Fred Darby*)

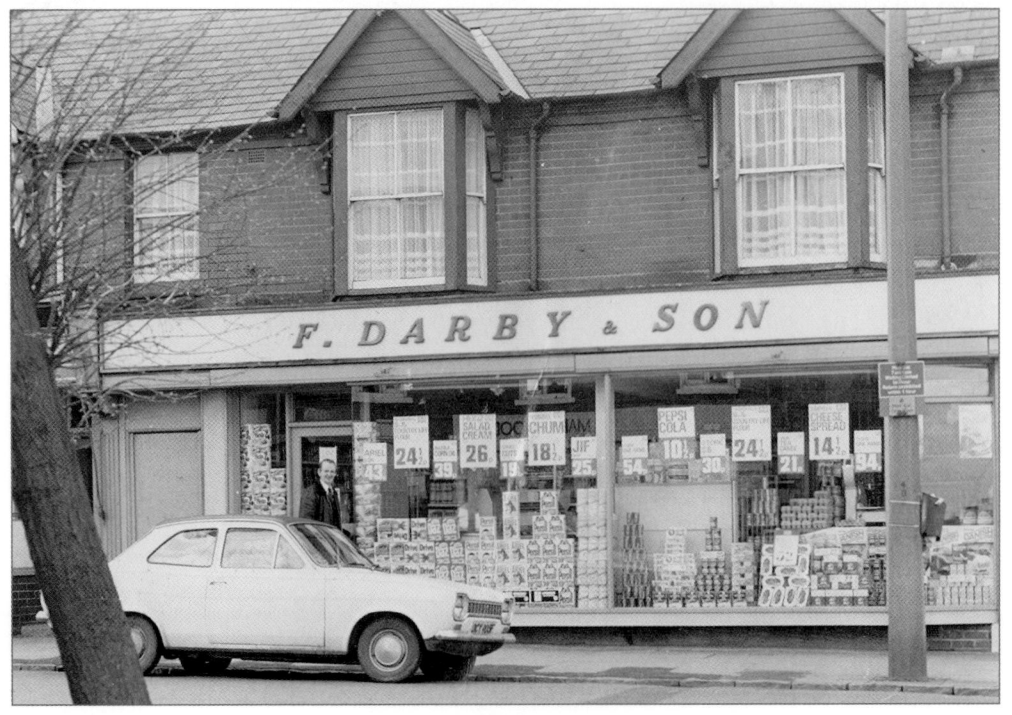

Faced by increasing competition from the smaller supermarkets, Fred decided to go 'self-service' in 1954, and the shop underwent a complete face-lift. (*Fred Darby*)

A fine display of luggage outside R. Cutler's premises at 110 High Street, 1960s. He also offered a boot and shoe repair service. (*Author*)

Brian and Sidney Churchill outside the family furniture shop in Halesowen Street, just before it was demolished in October 1996. The business had been in the family for three generations, having been established in 1899 by Mr Noah Churchill and his wife Annie. Personal service became the philosophy, and even customers who had moved out of the area came back with their orders. (*Brian Churchill*)

Ivy Shaw and Horace Taylor on the steps of the Taylors' shop in Hackett Street, 1919. At this time the shop owner was listed as Samuel Sturman, cowman and grocer, who later moved on to become a farmer in Beeches Road. Hackett Street was later renamed Heath Street, owing to popular demand after a celebrated murder happened there. (*Horace Taylor*)

Birmingham Road from the traffic island, 1969. At this time the Shoulder of Mutton was an Ansell's public house. (*C.H.A.S.*)

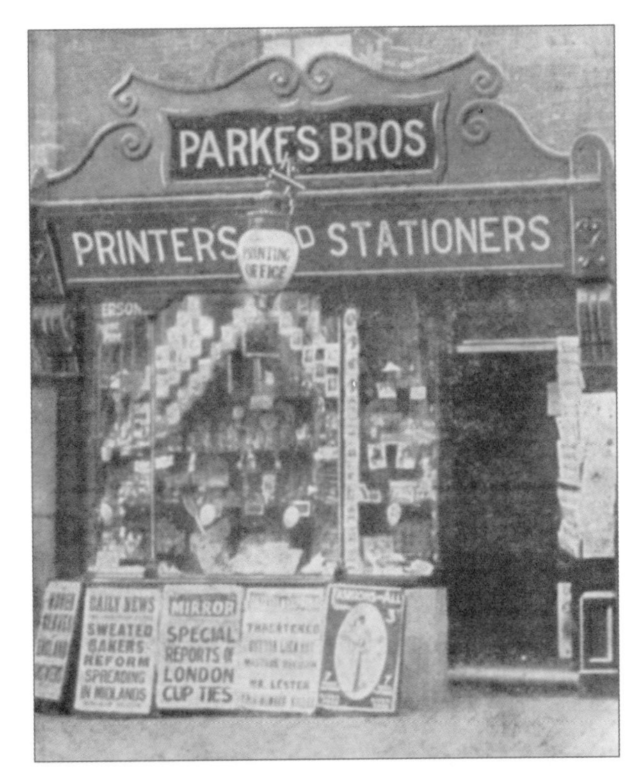

An advertisement for Parkes Bros, printers and stationers, 1915. Their shop was in High Street. Contemporary headlines can be read on the billboards, with the *Daily Mirror* reporting on the results of the London cup ties. Parkes was responsible for the production and distribution of postcards of the area, many of which are included in the early chapters of this book. (*Fred Darby*)

Jenny Nock behind the counter of the Bandbox, in the late 1950s. Situated next to the post office, it was originally founded as a music shop (see p. 98), selling both instruments and sheet music as well as giving music lessons, but the proprietors soon saw the advantage of moving into stationery because many people needed supplies when posting letters, or found it convenient to purchase a greetings card, fill it in and dispatch it next door. (*Les Nock*)

Fred Westwood posing with his daughter Linnie (who later emigrated to South Africa) and May Hughes (left), outside his fish and chip shop at the top of Oldbury Road. Inside the shop is Fred's wife Polly, who was heavily pregnant at the time and would not pose for the camera. The firm prided itself on fresh fish daily, collected from the wholesale market early each morning. The building on the left was the Bulls Head public house, which was closed down by the police shortly after this picture was taken, allegedly because of continued unruly behaviour. The passageway between the buildings led to the market. (*Polly Fletcher*)

John Tooth's builders merchants, mid-1950s. Their premises stood at the corner of High Street and Ross, and the adjacent cottages were soon demolished to allow easier access to Tooth's yard. (*John Tooth*)

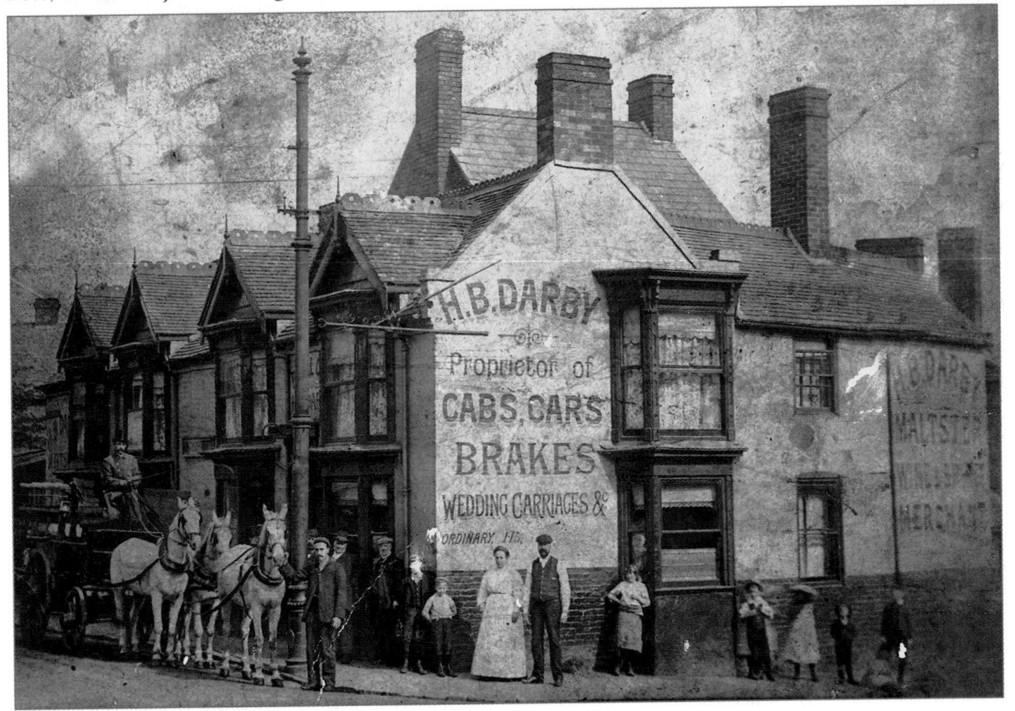

An unusual three-horse coach waits outside the Royal Oak, *c.* 1910. The snug bar and toilets were to be found on the side of the building facing Halesowen Street. (*Fred Darby*)

Grace Horton in the doorway of her shop in Halesowen Street, *c.* 1920. She was a very kind-hearted lady, who ran a 'slate' system for easy payment; it was common knowledge that she would not let a family go without food for the week, even if they had nothing with which to pay. (*Iris Dickens*)

The original Gate Inn at Whiteheath stood on the opposite corner to the present Gate Inn. Note the Midland Red timetable on the corner wall. This picture was taken in September 1959, when the beer was supplied by Butlers. (*Christopher Willetts*)

Mr and Mrs Wright outside their house in Fairfield Road in the 1960s. Mrs Wright ran the shop which offered teas, home-made ices, confectionery and a delicatessen, while her husband operated a dairy and milk delivery business from the yard behind the double gates. (*David Taylor*)

Fred Darby Snr opened his first grocery shop on a site opposite the market. His display includes a wide variety of cooked meats, and there are advertisements for Madame 'X' cakes and Firkins pork pies. The Darbys were involved in the Blackheath Operatic Society, and the current production at the King's Theatre in 1926 was 'The Dancing Mistress'. (*Fred Darby*)

Jane Eley opened her drapery business in High Street in the early part of the twentieth century, in premises adjacent to her brother's butcher's shop. Note the elaborate lantern over the entrance and the outside display of hats and corsets. Just peeking through on the extreme right of the picture is a youngster, perhaps a member of the family, who has spotted the photographer at work. (*Ros Hill*)

4

Churches & Chapels

An artist's drawing of the proposed Methodist New Connexion Church, Birmingham, prepared by the architects Ewen Harper & Bro. of Birmingham. The church society was originally formed in 1840 in a cottage in Yew Tree Lane, before moving on to hold services in Dr Beasley's coach-house in Siviters Lane. In 1849 the society purchased, for £5, some land in the Causeway where they built the Ebenezer Chapel, opened in 1850. The foundation stone of the church shown here was laid in October 1905 and it opened a year later in October 1906. A contemporary newspaper report indicated that all nine hundred seats were filled at the opening ceremony, with another thousand or so people unable to get in. (*Author's Collection*)

Crowds gathered in Park Street in August 1908 to witness the laying of the foundation stones for the new Citadel for the Salvation Army. (*Harry Jones*)

A few years earlier, in 1900, the Congregational Church in Green Lane was officially opened. This building was one of the first examples of 'flat-pack' construction. It soon became known as 'the tin chapel', for obvious reasons, and is still in use nowadays as the meeting place for Age Concern. The foundation stone for the brick-built church was laid in 1906. (*Sylvia Parkes*)

The parish church of St Paul occupies an area bordered by Long Lane, Church Street and the railway line. The foundation stone was laid by the Countess of Dudley on 18 April 1868, and the church was consecrated by Bishop Philpotts on 4 February 1869. Several major repairs had to be carried out within a few years because of subsidence from nearby mining and quicksand seeping on to the railway cutting. The tower was originally intended to be 100ft high, but this scheme was never implemented; indeed the small tower visible in this postcard had to be removed when it became unsafe. (*Colin Wood*)

The interior of St Paul's in the late 1920s, shortly after the introduction of electricity. The stone reredos was erected in 1897 in memory of the Revd F. Keatch, who had been vicar of the parish for twenty-four years, and the stained-glass window commemorating the coronation of King Edward VII was installed in 1902. (*Iris Dickens*)

The Revd G.K.M. Green (right) began his appointment as vicar of St Paul's in February 1907. With the assistance of the Revd H.A. Walke (left) and the Revd A.D. Stratford (centre), he conducted both morning and evening services on a daily basis, as well as engaging in many other functions which kept their diaries full. (*Revd David Garner*)

The Methodist Church was represented in the town by two Circuits, one of the Primitive tradition and the other of the New Connexion. The main Primitive church was in High Street. The original building (shown here) stood on the corner of High Street and John Street, and was constructed in 1850. It was demolished in 1951 to make way for a new primary department. (*Bert Cockin*)

High Street Methodist Church was built in 1902 at a cost of £7,000 and occupied a prime site at the top of the shopping area. It closed for worship on 28 December 1995 when it merged with several others to form the Central Church. It is the intention of the Blackheath Circuit to build a new church with community facilities at this location. (*Sheila Brookes*)

The choir of St Paul's Church pictured outside the main entrance to the church with the vicar, the Revd Ernest Bevan, in preparation for a Sunday School Festival service in June 1950. (*Mary Hackett*)

Mrs Martha Parkes lays one of the foundation stones for the new Sunday School building on the site of the Ebenezer Chapel, Causeway, in 1932. The church is in the background. (*David Taylor*)

St Paul's Church youth club, 1947. Back row, left to right: P. Dickens, G. Hadley, G. Hadley, C. Wood, J. Wilcox, J. Woodhall, I. Biggs, D. Dankey, J. Roberts, N. Biddle, L. Sidaway, T. Clarke, H. Pugh. Middle row: U. Clay, I. Taylor, L. Rollason, R. Blackwell, D. Taylor, M. Cole, D. Brown, -?-, -?-, M. Brookes, E. Holland, B. Chatwin, I. Gould, I. Wood, R. Bowling, D. Churchill, -?-, -?-. Front row: J. Bolton, C. Duffield, H. Roberts, J. Clarke, Revd E. Bevan, B. Dickens, E. Turbefield, E. Edwards, A. Higgs. Seated: L. Sidaway, R. Duffield, J. Clarke, J. Dickens, G. Skelding, R. Hadley, E. Blunt, A. Jones. (*Iris Dickens*)

The Revd C.L. Bannister was the second vicar of St Paul's and served between February 1894 and April 1897. He was described as an unpopular preacher although his sermons were very instructive and helpful to the spiritually minded. Before coming to Blackheath he had worked as a missionary in South Africa. (*David Garner*)

The Revd Albert Tattersall, minister at Birmingham Road Methodist Church from 1909 to 1914. (*Sheila Jones*)

The choir and clergy of St Paul's Church, photographed on the lawn of the old vicarage early in the twentieth century. (*David Garner*)

Sunday School pupils at the school's anniversary celebrations at High Street Methodist Church in 1938. (*Jim Brookes*)

The choir of St Ambrose Mission Church, Gorsty Hill, seen here with the organist, Edgar Brown, outside the church in the early 1950s. (*Margaret Williamson*)

Hurst Green Methodist Church in Narrow Lane was built in 1900, having been founded as a society ten years earlier. When a new church was built on adjacent land in 1936, this building was used as the Sunday School hall. (*Rita Shaw*)

The opening of the new church at Hurst Green, 4 February 1937. Right to left: Mr W. Higgins, Mrs H. Parkes, Miss Enid Higgins, Revd Albert Cole, Revd F.H. Benson, Mr E. Brookes. (*Rita Shaw*)

One of the highlights of the year was the annual Whit Sunday procession, when most of the churches in the area brought out their banners and marched towards a central spot, where games were held and the contents of the 'treat bag' were distributed. Here we see members of Gorsty Hill Methodist Church climbing the hill into Blackheath. (*Jim Brookes*)

A popular destination for the processions was Britannia Park, and here members of High Street church are seen approaching the park gates. Active people walked all the way, but most churches hired lorries from local firms to carry the younger children and pensioners, as can be seen on the extreme right. (*Mary Brookes*)

This assembly took place in Park Street, behind the market. The Salvation Army band generally accompanied the hymn singing and the marching. (*Frank Wyle*)

Dick Smith, the Primary Superintendent of High Street Methodist Sunday School, pictured in 1950 with children who had purchased bricks to be included in the new schoolroom. (*Bert Cockin*)

The Methodist church at Cocksheds had a fine organ, which was refurbished during 1950 by Messrs Noterman of Shepherds Bush, London. As part of the subsequent celebrations a celebrity concert was given to a full church by 'Mr Blackpool' himself, Reginald Dixon, on 6 July 1950. (*Norman Hurley*)

There were two Methodist churches in Malt Mill Lane, Cocksheds at the top and Malt Mill Lane at the bottom. This is the latter, which was first built in 1894. It closed for worship on 20 October 1995, when five congregations merged to form the new Blackheath Central Church. A new housing development now stands on this site. (*Christopher Willetts*)

Whiteheath Methodist Church was established in Birchfield Lane in 1842, and moved to these premises on the opposite side of the road in 1956. It, too, closed for worship in 1995 as part of the reorganisation, but the building remains very largely the same, and is now used as the headquarters for the local St John Ambulance Brigade. (*Christopher Willetts*)

The combined congregations came together in January 1996. Until the construction of their new church, they held their services in the former Birmingham Road United Methodist Church. Note the steep steps of the house next to the church, and the sweet shop next door, owned at one time by the Dalling family. (*Ken Rock Collection*)

The first steps towards the creation of Church of England day schools in Blackheath were taken in June 1871, when fundraising was started by the vicar, the Revd F. Keatch. Land in Long Lane was purchased from the Great Western Railway (with the portion over the railway tunnel only leased!), and Mr A.H. Allen was appointed the first master. The school was opened by the Earl and Countess of Dudley on 15 April 1873. St Paul's Court, a sheltered housing development, currently occupies the site. (*C.H.A.S.*)

The pupils of Birmingham Road Sunday School performing a pantomime in the 1950s. Among the pupils identified are Robert Dunn, Malcolm Ward, Christopher Wright, Ann Cutler, Joan Bennett, Patricia Jones and Wendy Ingram. (*Ann Harris*)

The interior of High Street Methodist Church in 1912, showing the pulpit, choir stalls and organ. The church was built to seat nine hundred people. (*Kath Mole*)

On 26 October 1867 a Trust Deed was drawn up establishing the formation of Hackett Street Methodist Church, and suitable land was purchased for £34. The Bethesda Wesleyan Reform Chapel was opened in 1875, and remained until the Heath Street clearance in 1976, when a new church was constructed on the opposite side of the road. (*Eric Parkes*)

The young people of Birmingham Road perform another pantomime, this time 'Aladdin'. (*Author's Collection*)

As part of their fundraising activities, members of High Street Methodist Church held a 'Victorian Evening' in 1973. Left to right: Gladys Andrews, Amy Brettle, Joan Turnbull, Carolyn Cockin, Sheila Brookes, Mary Parkes, Agnes Bagley, Lilian Price, the Revd George Price. (*Bert Cockin*)

A group of Methodists pictured at one of their garden parties at Highbury. Standing, left to right: Edward Whitehouse, Cyril Whorton, ? Payne, Harry Chambers, -?-, ? Mole, Norman Brettle, Charles Wright. Seated: Amy Brettle, Maisy Chambers, -?-, ? Wright, -?-, -?-. (*Amy Bussey*)

Cottage meetings were held at a house in Gorsty Hill until a disused Baptist chapel was rented as the Mission Church of St Paul's. In 1897 the Mission received notice to quit the chapel, and rooms were donated at Coombs Wood by Messrs Lloyd & Lloyd. The foundation stone for the St Ambrose Mission Church was laid on 24 July 1897, and it was used for the first time in September 1898 for a bazaar to raise funds to form another Mission in Waterfall Lane. (*Margaret Williamson*)

The large brass lectern of St Ambrose Mission Church was dedicated on 1 January 1899, together with a Bible presented by the Halesowen Lodge of Freemasons. Several years later the eagle was stolen by burglars and destroyed; many pieces were later found scattered around the district. (*Margaret Williamson*)

High Street Methodist Church, as seen from Darby Street. The caretaker's house stands next to the church. (*Christopher Willetts*)

Uniformed organisations have a long history as training grounds for young people of both sexes, and this is the Boys' Brigade of High Street Methodist Church pictured in 1947. (*Jim Brookes*)

Ladies have supported many local churches over the years, and these two photographs show the Birmingham Road Women's Own society in 1928 (top) and 1955 (below). In 1928 the minister was the Revd Thomas Jukes, and in 1955 it was the Revd John T. Gray. Many of the ladies in the lower picture are the daughters, or grand-daughters, of those in the upper one. (*Kath Mole/Frank Wyle*)

A report in the *Daily Mirror* in 1949 commented on the work of the Birmingham Road Mothers & Toddlers Group, said to be one of the first in the country, and it bore the headline 'Mothers Pray While Children Play'. Among the mothers and helpers pictured here are Estella Hancox, Lily Smith, Kath Mole, Polly Fletcher, Cath Wright and Emily Ingram. (*Polly Fletcher*)

Birmingham Road Youth Club presented a concert in the 1950s, and the performers included Graham Morgan, Peter Jones, Margaret Bagley, Dorothy Greening, Doreen Parkes, Velma Willetts, Marlene Haddleton, Barbara Jones, Ray Holmes, Margaret While, Joe Johnson and Geoffrey Wootton. (*David Taylor*)

A scene from the Birmingham Road Operatic Group's production of 'The Quaker Girl'. Left to right: Hilda Rose, John C. Hussey, Jack Parkes, Evelyn Careless, Miss Hobbs, Ray Truman. (*Frank Wyle*)

Shortly after the end of the Second World War, members of the Birmingham Road Men's Fireside Fellowship organised a trip to Alton Towers and are pictured relaxing in the gardens. Quite what they would make of the current theme park is open to question. Among the men seen here are Albert Willetts, Wesley Dunn, Bert Harris, Ernest Parkes, John Payne, Ernest Wyle, Albert Haddleton and Fred Adams. (*Frank Wyle*)

'Seated one day at the organ. . .'. Jim Brookes at the console of the organ at High Street Methodist Church in 1954. (*Charles Male*)

Jim Brookes again, this time at the Hammond organ, taking part in a musical marathon, one of his regular fundraising activities in the 1960s. He is kept going with food and drink provided by his wife Sheila, and watched over by Fred Smith and Bert Cockin. (*County Express*)

These young people, all dressed in their best clothes, had assembled for the Sunday School Anniversary at Birmingham Road Methodist Church in 1955. For many years the children were trained by the organist, Mr Frank Green, who was reputed to be a perfectionist. No talking was allowed, and all words, both spoken and sung, had to be learned by heart, so that no paper was visible to the large congregations (all of whom had the words in front of them in booklets!). (*Author's Collection*)

Thomas Howard Smith (1891–1964), commonly known as 'Uncle Howard', was leader of the Primary Department at Birmingham Road for many years, and he is seen here with Mrs Smith on his retirement from that post. The children are Robert Smith, Maria Aldridge, Mary Lynn Aldridge, Christopher Wright, Janet Mole and Wendy Ingram. (*Kath Mole*)

UNITED METHODIST CHURCH

BIRMINGHAM ROAD, BLACKHEATH.

CHRISTMAS SUNDAY

DECEMBER 21st, 1930

"THE MESSIAH"

10-45, 2-30 and 6 o'clock, Principals:

MADAME EMILY BROUGHTON

Soprano

MISS DORIS HAMILTON.

Contralto

MR. WEBSTER BOOTH

Tenor (London).

MR ARTHUR WRIGGLESWORTH.

Bass (Lichfield Cathedral).

Conductor—

MR. JOSEPH ADAMS,

Organist—

MR. ERNEST PARKES,

Chairman - COUNCILLOR B. HOBBS.

Short Address at the evening Service by the Minister

Generous Collections are asked to reduce the adverse balance on Trust Funds

PARKES BROS., PRINTERS, BLACKHEATH.

The annual performance of Handel's *Messiah*, when the Birmingham Road choir would be augmented by other local singers, became a local musical tradition. Special guest stars were invited to perform as principal singers, and over the years many notable artists have performed this role. In this programme from 1930, the tenor was Webster Booth, who went on to become a very popular international duettist with his wife Anne Ziegler in later years. John Hanson, of 'Desert Song' fame, was another tenor soloist. A hundred performances were given before the tradition sadly terminated in the late 1990s. (*Lily Smith*)

5

Work & Play

Staff at Stewarts & Lloyds steel works, Coombs Wood, carry on working with their shop decked out in patriotic bunting to mark the coronation of Queen Elizabeth II in 1953. (*Valerie Lloyd*)

The mine at Rowley Hall colliery was connected via a rope-worked inclined railway (above) to the canal wharf and basin at Whiteheath (below), where the coal was loaded by hand into the waiting barges for distribution. These pictures were taken in about 1900. (*C.H.A.S.*)

British Thompson Houston (BTH) was a major employer. The company originally made electric motors, and here we see shaft production in 1923. (*Tony Houghton*)

Long before the days of sexual equality most factories had separate areas in which men and women were allowed to take their breaks. This is the men's canteen at BTH in 1923. (*Tony Houghton*)

Festivals and carnivals have always been popular in the town and early in the twentieth century the Blackheath Ambulance Carnival was one of the highlights of the year. Here we see Major, Harry and Lucy Darby outside the snug bar of the Royal Oak, as they prepare to take their decorated pony and trap to join the procession. (*Fred Darby*)

Jack Rose began working for John Tooth at his business in High Street in 1918, when he was just thirteen, and graduated to driving the firm's Bean delivery lorry (pictured here outside the shop). He worked there for fifty-one years, retiring in 1969. (*Ken Rose*)

The lorries of Adam Jones & Son are a familiar sight around the country these days but when the business was originally established in Ashley Street in about 1900 it had just one horse-drawn trailer. Pictured (right) outside the family home is Joe Nock, a mechanic with the firm, and a Thorneycroft lorry in 1949. Below: a few years later, in 1972, two lorries are loaded with tubes at Stewarts & Lloyds by Peter Jones and John Parkes. (*John Jones*)

One of the most popular entertainers in the West Midlands (and further afield) for many years was the accordionist Les Devaldi, who appeared at all sorts of events, from children's parties through to major variety performances. He was a member of the Variety Artistes' Federation, and appeared with many top-flight personalities throughout his career. He is pictured here in one of his routines in about 1950. (*Les Nock*)

In addition to being a performer, Les Devaldi was also a music teacher from the age of eighteen, and he formed some of his pupils into the Junior Band in 1949. They entered and won most of the major championships in the country. The members of the band were Les Devaldi, Johnny Alan, Susan Sayce, Barry Smith, Mack Hadley, Royston Taylor, Bruce Rollinson, Gerald Oakley, Graham Jaynes, Henry Steele, Brian Oakley, Stephen Watton, Brian Taylor, Trevor Parkes, Doug Yardley, Harry Hanson and Hewitt Cartwright. (*Eric Watton*)

The employees of Housing Limited formed their own jazz band, which performed at local events. They are seen here posing in their costumes ready for the Blackheath Carnival in 1932. (*Chris Willetts*)

Before the days of global travel and package holidays, the annual works outing was an event to anticipate with relish. These well-turned-out employees of T.W. Lench are enjoying a boat-trip on the River Thames at Windsor in the late 1940s. (*Mary Hackett*)

This rare picture of an early cricket team shows the elegant group who played their matches in Britannia Park in the early 1900s. The only identified player is John Taylor, holding the bat on the front row. (*Horace Taylor*)

Although they were not exactly Blackheath's answer to The Beatles, these three members of the Les Devaldi Junior Band had formed their own group, The Echoes, and performed successfully at many charity functions, often raising considerable funds. Left to right: Brian Taylor, Steve Watton, Brian Oakley. (*Author's Collection*)

T.W. Lench was justly proud of the range of activities that the firm provided for its employees, not least the Excelsior Band, which played at functions throughout the district. (*Ken Rock Collection*)

The formation of the Blackheath Male Choir was perhaps influenced by the influx of men from Shropshire and South Wales who came to the Midlands to find employment in the mines and the steel works. Little is known of the choir's early history, but they must have achieved a high

It is thought that this football team of around 1920 was based in a coffee house in Oldbury Road, and played their home fixtures in the same area. (*Frank Wyle*)

standard because they are seen here after performing in the Welsh National Eisteddfod in August 1919, held that year in Corwen. (*Kath Mole*)

The Stewarts & Lloyds St John Ambulance Brigade was inspected in 1963 on the works recreation ground. Back row, left to right: H. Shotton, B. Bingham, N. Hurley, E. Hipkiss, F. Harrison, A. Tromans, G. Crompton, J. Davies, T. Page. Front row: F. Hingley, three area officers, Dr Haigh, F. Harris, A. Pearson, W. Hipkiss, D. Payne. (*Charles Male*)

To celebrate the presentation of long-service awards to several employees at Lench's, the entire company sat down to a meal and entertainment in the men's canteen on 9 February 1952. (*Darren Bagley*)

The fire brigade of the Blackheath Works of BTH Ltd, proudly displaying the trophies they had gained in competition, including the Stafford Corporation Perpetual Challenge Shield (right). Left to right: J. Swain, -?-, A. Cannon Snr, A. Cannon Jnr, F. Willetts. (*Tony Houghton*)

The mason works on one of the last memorials to be produced at Dallows Monumental Ltd in Avenue Road, prior to closure in 1973. (*Ron Wood*)

This *County Express* photograph shows the first presentation of gold watches to long-service employees of Belgrave (Blackheath) Ltd, which took place at the Station Hotel, Dudley, in the 1980s. Mr Henry Pittaway, chairman of the company, is in the centre of the front row. (*Mary Hackett*)

The St John Ambulance Brigade of Stewarts & Lloyds, pictured in 1920. (*Colin Wood*)

T.W. Lench Ltd's award-winning football team of 1923/4. (*Colin Wood*)

Blackheath United Methodist football club, 1924/5. Many young men joined the church at this time simply to become part of the football team, which was quite a successful one, winning many local competitions. The bearded gentleman at the back is Mr J. Steward (Sunday School Superintendent). On the left of the middle row is James Page, whose son Arthur (team mascot) is on the extreme right of the back row. On the left of the front row is Albert Willetts, with Ernest Wyle on the extreme right. Both Arthur and Ernest went on to complete over forty years each as local preachers. (*Frank Wyle*)

British Thompson Houston Ltd's premises were built in 1917 as a government munitions and cartridge factory, and the entire workforce is pictured here outside the main building in that year. (*Phyllis Bateman*)

The works of Thomas Gadd's rivet-making firm stood opposite T.W. Lench's factory in Ross. It is now the site of a small residential development. (*Ron Wood*)

An aerial view of the British Thompson Houston factory, which began making electric motors in Blackheath in 1920. The picture highlights the rural nature of Cakemore and Hurst Green at the time, with extensive farming still taking place where now housing estates and industrial developments are the norm. (*Tony Houghton*)

On most Saturday evenings in the years between 1920 and 1939 a crowd would gather outside the George and Dragon in High Street. Most weeks there would be an ox roast (top), with visits by entertainers such as jugglers and often a dancing bear. In the lower picture Ben Hobbs is seen waiting for the roast to begin, watched by a small boy sitting on the roof of the pub's toilets. (*Author's Collection/Ivy Hall*)

A young Les Devaldi pictured with his partner Bernard Robinson, with whom he opened the Bandbox shop in High Street (see p. 49). (*Les Nock*)

The Lion Works football team. The factory was situated at the bottom of Waterfall Lane and was connected to Stewarts & Lloyds of Coombs Wood. This picture dates from around 1910, and the only identified person is Joseph Wyle, standing to the left of the goalkeeper. (*Frank Wyle*)

Joseph Newman and two colleagues at work on the building of the new dairy distribution centre for Midland Counties Dairies Ltd, Long Lane. The up-to-date concrete mixer gives some idea of the physical labour that was involved in the construction industry at the time. (*Morris Newman*)

The principal singers in the production of 'Pearl, the Fisher Maiden', staged by the Birmingham Road Operatic Group in 1927/8. Back row, left to right: Bill Southall, Frank Honeysett, Olive Laing, Howard Bannister, Frank Parsons. Front row: -?-, -?-, Ada Adams, Linnie Westwood. (*Ethel Southall*)

The works canteen at Belgrave (Blackheath) Ltd, specially prepared for the Christmas party for employees' children in 1954. (*Mary Hackett*)

The Blackheath Operatic Society presented Gilbert & Sullivan's 'HMS Pinafore' in a performance at the Pavilion Theatre, High Street, in November 1915. The principals were Alec Thomson, George Wall, Fred Clifford, Harry Preedy, W.J. Munslow, J. Holden, Arthur Roberts, Miss Annie Hadley, Mrs Alec Thomson and Mrs George Harris. Admission was priced between 6*d* and 1/6*d*, with an extra 3*d* for early seats. (*Fred Darby*)

Jim Field working on an early motor vehicle at his garage in Station Lane (now Nimmings Road). He went on to establish a successful motor-coach business. (*Iris Lee*)

In common with many factories, British Thompson Houston Ltd had its own railway sidings linked to the main railway system. Engines like this little shunter were used to collect components and to deliver finished products. (*Tony Houghton*)

A group of Blackheath ladies dressed in their finery for a day trip in a soft-topped charabanc. The driver, on the left of the group, was the proprietor Stanley Field. (*Iris Lee*)

After a gap of some years, the Blackheath Carnival was once again held in 1960. The procession is seen here near the Beech Tree public house at the top of Halesowen Street, led by the carnival queen and her attendants in an open-topped American car. (*Ken Jackson*)

6

People & Events

Ron Whyley represented the Blackheath Ward as Labour councillor from 1980 to 1997, and was elected to the position of Mayor of Sandwell in 1988. Until his untimely death, he lived in Shepherds Fold with his wife Janet. In this official portrait he is seen in the robes of office. (*Sydney Darby & Son*)

Ernest Honeysett Snr is obviously proud of his new delivery van, as he has driven it from the family business premises on Shell Corner to visit his sister, who had married a farmer and lived near Evesham, Worcs. The journey must have been something of an ordeal, given the vehicle's solid wheels and the un-made state of the roads in those days. (*Ernest Honeysett*)

John T. Hughes (left), pictured in uniform in 1915. In his youth he was a good footballer and played for several local teams, even gaining a trial with Aston Villa FC. His future lay elsewhere, though, as he was later ordained as a Methodist minister and travelled the length of the country in his appointments. (*Ray Holmes*)

Seen behind their home and shop premises in High Street, Ben Hobbs and family pose for the annual group photograph, which was sent to friends and relatives. The stock of building material stored in the yard attests to the nature of the business. Mr Hobbs was the first charter mayor of the Rowley Regis Borough Council, with Mrs Hobbs as his mayoress, in 1933. (*Iris Harrold*)

Answering Kitchener's call to arms, Fred Westwood left his fish and chip shop to serve in the First World War, and here he is resplendent on horseback during his period of training. (*Barbara Holmes*)

Ethel Waters, jokingly referred to by the family as 'the milk woman', is seen here with Prince the dog as she carries the churns along the path beside Whiteheath Villa. The lane led past the houses in the distance to the main Blackheath–Oldbury Road. (*Ann Willetts*)

Decimus Gaunt, commonly known as 'Jess', was the landlord of The Old Bush Revived in Powke Lane for more than fifty years, and he is seen here with some of his pals outside the public house in the late nineteenth century. He was the father of thirteen children and his eldest son Percival went on to found the famous family firm of undertakers. (*Peter Gaunt*)

John Tooth (left) with two colleagues aboard the SS *Otranto* in the North Sea in 1928. He started his working life as a painter and decorator in West Bromwich in the 1890s, but realising the opportunities Blackheath offered he moved his family and business to the top of High Street. He continued in the painting trade, although it soon became clear that there was more profit to be made from selling builders' materials, so he opened the shop and yard which remained in the family until recent times. (*John Tooth*)

A group photograph taken at the wedding of May Hughes and Harry Jones, 5 April 1926. The reception took place in the garden at the Hughes's family home in Oldbury Road. The bride is featured on the cover of this publication, and the minister was her brother John. (*Barbara Holmes*)

Blackheath Nursing Division in the 1930s, photographed at a garden party held in the grounds of the home of Miss Nellie Lench in Waterfall Lane, in appreciation of the nursing duties they carried out at the Guest Hospital, Dudley. Back row, left to right: Rose Wilkins, Irene Pritchard, Agnes Bagley, Nellie Lench, Nora Neil, Elsie Barrett, Mary Dickens. Front row: Mabel Hooper, Margaret Taylor, Elizabeth Ashman, Ann Homer, 'Bobbie' Norday, Annie Southall. ('Bobbie' Norday ran Bobbies' Ladies Lingerie Shop in High Street, Blackheath; she was French and always had the latest fashions). (*Irene Pritchard*)

The Blackheath Sons of Rest pictured in Green Lane in the 1940s. It must have been a special occasion, because their headquarters was in Britannia Park where there was plenty of space for such photographs to be taken. The Sons of Rest movement is thought to have started in Birmingham in the 1920s and quickly spread through the area, attracting many men of retirement age. When this picture was taken the president was Mr Jones, seated in the centre of the front row. The two ministers are the Revd Gordon Webb (left) and the Revd Walter Cooper (right), the latter of Blackheath origin. They continued to meet in the park until a purpose-built hall was opened in Rowley village in 1957. (*Barbara Honeysett*)

A miners' strike in 1912 brought hardship to many families, and in this emotive picture we see women and children of the area picking scraps of coal from the open-cast workings. (*C.H.A.S.*)

Ernest Parkes was one of the children of Benjamin and Hannah Parkes from Darby Street. Born in 1883, he joined his father and brothers in the building trade. He was a lifelong member of the Methodist church at Birmingham Road, and was a Trustee for many years. His brother Herbert, born in 1888, entered local politics and later became a county alderman for Worcestershire. He is seen (below) with his wife Martha in their robes as Mayor and Mayoress of Halesowen in 1947. Ernest and Herbert, with their brother Samuel James and four other men, each staked £100 to start Housing Limited, with premises opposite the station. Among other projects, this company built the Blackheath Odeon in Long Lane and much of the residential housing in the town. (*David Taylor*)

The Sons of Rest meet in the schoolroom of Birmingham Road Methodist Church to celebrate their Christmas dinner in the late 1950s. Mr J.W. Jones (president) is standing on the stage addressing the company. (*Frank Wyle*)

Amy Brettle has enjoyed a life-long association with the St John Ambulance Brigade. In recognition of her devotion she was elected to the position of Serving Sister, being presented with certificates and medals by members of the royal family. (*County Express*)

The Duke and Duchess of York visited the Black Country on Thursday 4 June 1925, and went to T.W. Lench's Excelsior Works, where the duke planted a tree (above) in the firm's garden of remembrance, assisted by the gardener Zachariah Ness. Twenty-seven fir trees were planted in the garden to commemorate the firm's employees killed in the First World War. Below: the royal couple with Mr Harry Lench as they take their leave of the factory. (*Robert Lench*)

Ellen Wood, pictured in the 1920s. She is standing on the opposite side of the road to her cottage in Oldbury Road. At the time there was a clear view across the fields up to Rowley Church. When the council estate was developed, Stilehouse Crescent, off Britannia Road, was so-named because it stood on the site of an old house with a stile, which would be somewhere in the middle distance of this picture. (*Colin Wood*)

Miss Nellie Lench JP performs the opening ceremony for a charity garden party, one of many which were held during the 1960s and 1970s in the grounds of Highbury, the home of Mr and Mrs Norman Brettle. (*Amy Bussey*)

The Adams family, pictured at home in December 1893. James Adams Snr was a well-known music teacher, exclusively using tonic solfa, and was in great demand by church choirs and other singers. He was a machine fitter by trade, and worked on one of the first machines to be set up at Lench's, where he was a foreman. (This earned him the nickname 'doggy Adams', the reason for which is not known.) (*Kath Mole*)

When the family moved into this house in Tump Road (now Beeches Road), Mr Adams named it Curwen Cottage after the London-based music firm that published the tonic solfa method. The name is still visible today in the lintel over the doorway. (*C.H.A.S.*)

The families of workers at British Thompson Houston get ready to enjoy a film show as part of their Christmas party in 1948. (*Darren Bagley*)

The VE-Day party in Heath Street, with locals lined up to serve the children, who seem to have started celebrating already. In common with many streets at this time, many local people opened small shops in their front rooms, as can be seen on the right. (*Freda Green*)

RAF personnel relaxing near Blackpool, where they were posted for training as wireless operators in the Second World War. Two of them were friends from Blackheath, Albert Evans (extreme left) and Ivan Green (third from right). Albert survived the war but Ivan was not so fortunate. (*Edna Cockin*)

Sergeant Ivan Green was killed in action on Sunday 21 September 1941, and was buried at St Giles's parish church following a service at High Street Methodist Church on Saturday 27 September. The streets were lined with people, and there was a commemorative fly-past in his honour. Here the cortège passes the George and Dragon, with the air raid shelter that faced Regis Road clearly visible. (*Peter Gaunt*)

Mr Gerry Westwood, the owner of the fish and chip shop next to the Market Place, pictured with an unidentified driver in one of his earlier vehicles in the early 1920s. (*Polly Fletcher*)

Alderman Ernest Gervase White represented the Blackheath ward on Warley County Borough Council, and was for many years chairman of the Housing Committee. He lived in Habberley Road, and was elected to be Mayor of Warley in 1972 and 1973. (*County Express*)

One of the principal providers of excursions for townsfolk was Branscombe's Coaches, a firm commonly known by the name of its proprietor, Florrie Dunn. She is seen here (on the second row, holding a handbag) with a group of ladies including Mrs Polly Westwood (second from left, back row) and Mrs Olive Wootton (centre), perhaps at Southport, during one of her outings. On most charabanc tours, part of the excitement was wondering whether there would be a breakdown during the trip! (*Polly Fletcher*)

The Loyal Order of Moose has always had a keen membership in the area. At one time there were two separate Lodges, but these combined to form Lodge 117, seen here at a function held at the Botanical Gardens, Edgbaston, in 1953. They originally held their meetings in the parochial hall in Vicarage Road but later obtained their own Moose Hall by purchasing the redundant Methodist Church in Beeches Road. (*Bert Cockin*)

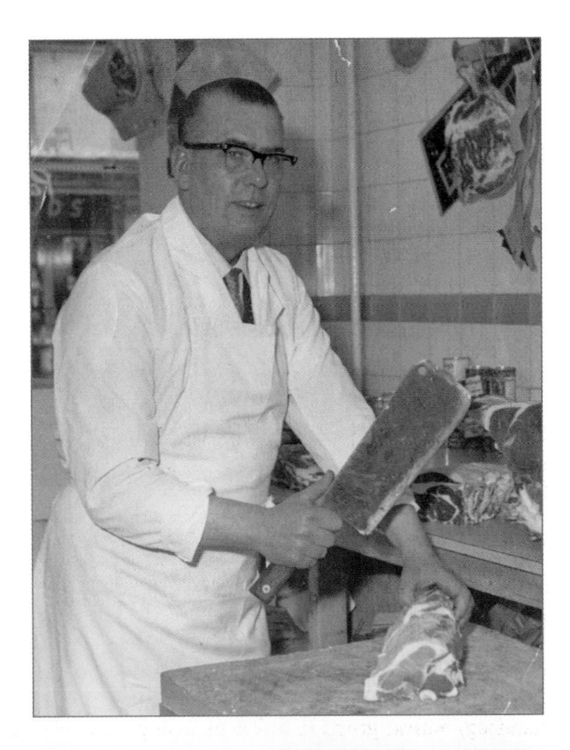

Fred Clift entered the butchery trade in 1928 when he left Beeches Road school, working first as a pork butcher then as assistant in Tom Darby's shop in High Street. After Darby's death in 1935 Fred purchased the business, expanding into the shop next door as trade picked up. It was a family concern and he was helped in the shop by his wife Eva, daughter Freda and son Michael. Fred was a member of the management committee, and later president, of the Blackheath Liberal Club. (*County Express*)

In 1945 members of Blackheath Labour Party and their families enjoyed a visit to the House of Commons, being given a guided tour by Mr Arthur Henderson, MP for Rowley Regis & Tipton (seen pointing). When he retired from the constituency, Henderson was elected to the House of Lords, taking the title Lord Rowley. (*Janet Whyley*)

Stephen (left) and Neil Harris in George Avenue, posing in front of the family's furniture van in 1959. The business was originally run from their home in Birmingham Road, but now operates in the former Methodist Sunday School, where it is run by Stephen and his elder brother Paul. (*Neil Harris*)

Opening of Midland Counties Dairy, Long Lane, 20 October 1949. Standing, second from right, is Dr R.L. Corlett, Halesowen's Medical Officer, with third from right Mr A. Archer, Chief Public Health Officer. Seated on the left are the Mayor and Mayoress of Halesowen, Cllr and Mrs A.G. Rudge. Seated on the right are the Mayor and Mayoress of Rowley Regis, Alderman and Mrs G.A. Palmer. (*David Eades*)

Stanley Field poses in front of *Lady Iris*, one of the fleet of Field coaches, in 1922 or 1923. His parents, Mr and Mrs Jim Field, are on the right. Jim and his brother had originally run a garage business but when they went their separate ways Jim formed the coach firm, which he later handed on to Stanley. (*Iris Lee*)

Rowley Regis, previously administered by an Urban District Council within Staffordshire County Council, was granted a Charter of Incorporation to become a Borough in 1933. A commemorative mayoral procession through the streets was held on 28 September, and part of the gathering is seen here passing down High Street. (*C.H.A.S.*)

John Rose was a mechanic, and had garage premises in Halesowen Street. He was also one of the first people in the town to offer car-hire facilities. His wife Min is in the back of the car, pictured outside St Ambrose Mission Church, Gorsty Hill, in 1930. (*Iris Dickens*)

Rowley Regis Library Committee, 1965/6. Back row, left to right: Cllr John Padden, Cllr George Homer, Cllr Eric Bower, Ald. Samuel Walker. Middle row: Cllr Ernest White, Ald. Reg Downing, Cllr John Shakespeare, Cllr William Salt, Cllr George Shaw. Front row: Cllr Jack Lloyd, M.G. Cookson (town clerk), Ald. Evelyn Matthews JP (Mayor), Cllr Thomas Porter BA, Miss Anne Price (librarian), R.H. Scriven (borough architect). (*C.H.A.S.*)

The tables in Oldbury Road are well laden for the 1953 coronation celebrations, which took place in the garage premises of Mason's Coaches. (*Polly Fletcher*)

A good crowd of children and their parents gathered in May 1954 at the Stewarts & Lloyds Social Club in Coombs Wood to see Ray Barlow, captain of the cup-winning West Bromwich Albion football team, showing off the FA cup so that locals can have a closer look. (*County Express*)

George Smith in the doorway of his house in Darby Street, awaiting transfer to his new accommodation, as all around him the bulldozers flatten the old houses to make way for the new housing development. (*Roy Horton*)

The children of Birmingham Road in patriotic mood as they celebrate the coronation of Queen Elizabeth II in June 1953. Those present include Roger Connell, Neil Harris, Ann Cutler, Christine Siviter, Arlene Mann, Ronnie Mann, Stephen Harris, Rosemary Yates, Jean Coombes, Paul Harris, Tommy Groves, Edna Patrick, Mrs Smith, Mrs Cutler, Mrs Taylor, Mrs Bowater, Mrs Coombes, Mrs Howard, Janet Connell, Peter Bird, Jean Howard, Margaret Bradley, Gillian Partridge, Betty Cutler, John Groves, Jimmy Taylor, Doreen Holmes, John Tromans, Derek Taylor and Mrs Harris. (*Barbara Holmes*)

Some of the residents meet outside 9 Beeches Road for their VE-Day celebrations. Back row, left to right: Mr J. Ford, Mr L. Bloomer, Mr C. Potts, Mr B. Parsons. Middle row: Mr L. Adams, Mrs A. Parsons, Mrs Stoker, Mrs Bloomer, Mrs Stoker. Front row: Mrs E. Ford, Mrs Adams, Mrs Walker. Many of these people ran their own businesses in the Beeches Road area. (*Barry Parsons*)

Ron Whyley, Mayor of Sandwell, accompanied by Miss Sandwell, switches on the Blackheath Christmas lights in December 1988. (*County Express*)

A horse and trap follows the tram tracks in Holly Road in 1912, photographed from the corner of Beeches Road. Much of the housing on the right-hand side of the road remains to the present day, whereas the left-hand side has been cleared. (*Ken Rock Collection*)

The view down George Avenue (formerly Mott Street) in 1973, from the junction with Birmingham Road. The old corn mill on the right was constructed in 1904. The rear entrance to the coach station is visible at the end of the road. (*Ron Wood*)

ACKNOWLEDGEMENTS

Thanks are expressed to all those individuals and organisations who have loaned pictures for this publication. Wherever possible, photographs have been credited to the original photographer, but failing that to the person loaning the picture. Permission to use photographs has been sought where it has been possible to establish the copyright holder, but apologies are extended for any inadvertent breach of copyright.

Special thanks must be extended to Jeff Jephcott, Editor (*News Group*), for the use of photographs and material from the *County Express*; to Ken Rock and Tony Taylor for allowing me access to their postcard collections; to the staff of the *Black Country Bugle* for their continued cooperation; and to the staff of the Sandwell Community History and Archive Service (C.H.A.S.), especially Maureen Waldron, for their support and encouragement throughout this project.

The author intends to donate any royalties from this book to the building fund for the Blackheath Central Methodist Church, and would like to thank everyone who contributes to the appeal by purchasing this publication.

THE BLACK COUNTRY SOCIETY

This voluntary society, affiliated to the Civic Trust, was founded in 1967 as a reaction to the trend of the late 1950s and early 1960s to amalgamate everything into large units and in the Midlands to sweep away the area's industrial heritage in the process.

The general aim of the Society is to create interest in the past, present and future of the Black Country, and early on it campaigned for the establishment of an industrial museum. In 1975 the Black Country Living Museum was started by Dudley Borough Council on 26 acres of totally derelict land adjoining the grounds of Dudley Castle. This has developed into an award-winning museum which attracts over 250,000 visitors annually.

It was announced in August 1998 that having secured a lottery grant of nearly £3 million, the Museum Board will be able to authorize the start of work on a £4.5 million state-of-the-art interpretation centre. This will be known as the 'Rolfe Street Project', named after the street which once housed the Smethwick Baths. The façade of this Victorian building is to be incorporated into the new interpretation centre.

At the Black Country Living Museum there is a boat dock fully equipped to restore narrowboats of wood and iron and different vessels can be seen on the dock throughout the year. From behind the Bottle and Glass Inn visitors can travel on a canal boat into Dudley Canal Tunnel, a memorable journey to see spectacular limestone caverns and the fascinating Castle Mill Basin.

There are 2,500 members of the Black Country Society and all receive the quarterly magazine *The Blackcountryman*, of which 124 issues have been published since its founding in 1967. In the whole collection there are some 1,800 authoritative articles on all aspects of the Black Country by historians, teachers, researchers, students, subject experts and ordinary folk with an extraordinary story to tell. The whole constitutes a unique resource about the area and is a mine of information for students and researchers who frequently refer to it. Many schools and libraries are subscribers. Three thousand copies of the magazine are printed each quarter. It is non-commercial, and contributors do not receive payment for their articles.

PO Box 71 · Kingswinford · West Midlands DY6 9YN